Bells are metal.

metal

hammer

A bell has a
hammer, or 'clapper'.

The hammer hits the metal when the bell is rung.

Big bells hang in a steeple.

steeple

bell

Bell-ringers tug on the long, thick cords to ring the bells.

Bells ring at weddings.

Different sorts of bells:

finger bells

hand bells

foot bells

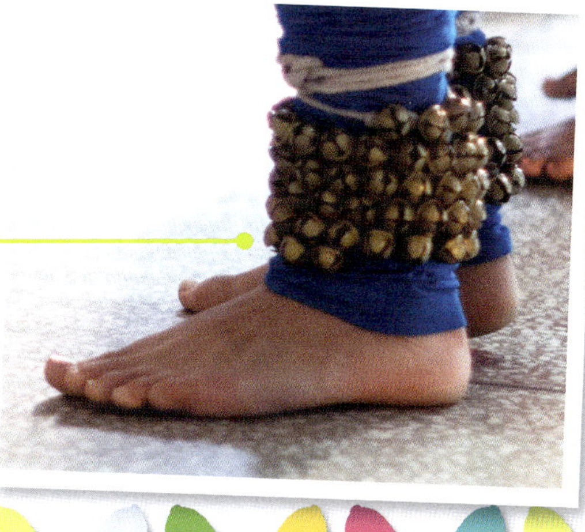

Big Ben

Big Ben is the bell,
not the clock.